Dear Shame,
Let's break up!

How to stay present inside of God's truth
and be set free from the torture
of false beliefs.

Lisa L. Roitsch

Dedication

I dedicate this book to my husband, William Joseph. You have loved me, despite all my shame, held my hand as I painfully explored it and given me the freedom to dream! Thank you for fully loving me and allowing me to be fully known. You are a real conqueror and you are still the ONE!

To our three daughters, Carissa, Loryn, and Kaleigh; I began this book years ago because I wanted to leave a piece of my story behind for you to finish. Run your race girls...never give up, and always remember, each of you are history makers! I love you.

To the reader:

My hope is that this book will open your eyes to the damaging effects of shame. It is not an exhaustive study, but merely a beginner's guide to healing. My prayer is that you will rise up, take courage and rip off the costume that covers shame. I sincerely hope that you will interact with this book, make notes and journal as you begin to discover new things about yourself and God. Grab a highlighter, a pen, an extra journal or two and have fun! Dare to discover your true self and begin enjoying who you truly are. Life is not only a journey but, with God, it is an exciting and unpredictable adventure!

CONTENTS

1. **Prologue**
2. **Shades of Shame** - all He has are broken people
3. **Coming Out of Your Wilderness** - a look back at shame in biblical times
4. **Make Pain Your Friend** - shine light on the darkness
5. **Identity Theft** - feelings and behavior are not who we really are
6. **Healing and Forgiveness** - real healing; a walk through the process of forgiveness
   a. Prayer of Forgiveness
   b. Declaration of Release
7. **Purpose and Passion** - God delights in you
8. **Finding Satisfaction** - allowing your soul to be restored
9. **A New Time and A New Place** - the promise of truth and peace
10. **Sow Well** - be intentional and reap abundantly
11. **Epilogue**

Prologue 1

In order to conquer any shame in our lives, we must learn to embrace where we are and come to a greater understanding of unconditional love. As long as we're only conditionally known, we'll only be conditionally loved. Until we are willing to be open and free, we will never experience the unconditional love that is waiting for us from a loving and forgiving God.

TO BE FULLY KNOWN IS TO BE FULLY LOVED

I know shame on many levels. I have seen and heard shame in counseling and walking beside many women and young girls who have suffered its devastating consequences. In my personal experiences, I have felt the death grip that shame puts on a soul.

My own story of shame came out of deep rejection and abandonment from my father and mother, as well as being sexually abused at a young age. It wasn't until I was into adulthood, and had children of my own, that I fully realized the condition I was in. My shame had become like putrid poison that swirled inside of my body and every time I was squeezed, some of it leaked out.

I grew up believing that any worth I had was based on my performance. At an early age, I came to believe that I needed to perform well in order to receive people's love and affection, especially my father's. My parents divorced while I was still a small child so I longed for my dad's approval from afar. If my strong need for approval was not met in huge doses, I learned to do whatever I needed to do in order to be loved. Breaking free from performing for others and from being a people pleaser has been a very long journey for me. The process began as I learned to accept and embrace who *Gods says* I am. The lies that swirled around inside of my brain were so loud; at times, it felt as though they were constantly yelling at me! The lies were so familiar to me that it was challenging to recognize them and separate them from the truth of God's Word.

Some of the lies sounded like this:

"If you say 'No' you are a bad person."

"You must earn God's approval, or He won't love you."

Because of the lies that I was believing, I was willing to do whatever it took to become a person that others would like. According to my view, in order to be liked I had to perform well and do things that made other people happy.

In my early 20s I began attending church and reading the bible. What this did was cause me to feel better about myself and fill my head with lots of knowledge. I was doing good works for God by serving, teaching children's Sunday school and attending lots of bible studies. However, somewhere I fell short of understanding that what I really needed was a deep and intimate relationship with the ONE who wrote the bible. The many bible verses I memorized puffed me up but did not carry the authority or power to quicken me or awaken me fully. I was merely checking off my "to do" list in order to please God and others and feel better about myself. I missed the point that what I desperately needed was a close, intimate relationship with my creator in order to walk in true and lasting freedom!

I love the verse in Philippians which states:

"….work out your own salvation with fear and trembling; for it is God who works IN YOU both to will and to do for His good pleasure."

(Philippians 2:12, NKJV)

This communicates to me that our on-going salvation is a process, a journey; a holy and separating process. It is coming out of shame, into honor, taking off the ashes of my past and putting on His beauty. I choose joy over sorrow, because I certainly cannot undo the past.

Over the years, I have ministered to and coached many women and men who have walked this path. I have led countless bible studies, but I always strive to encourage others to learn WHO the comforter is. The bible is more than just about knowledge or a history lesson. God is still living and working inside the pages of the book. It wasn't until I did a study years ago called <u>Breaking Free</u>, by Beth Moore, that I began to understand some of the concepts I will be sharing with you in this book. I remember the first time I read Isaiah 61 that shows us Jesus' mandate to heal our broken hearts. In this passage God reveals to us the powerful exchange He wants to bring to us.

Beauty for ashes, joy for our mourning and double honor for all our shame.

Wow! THAT is good news. If you have not read these scriptures, I urge you to begin reading all of chapter 61 in the book of Isaiah. God is all about bringing redemption and restoration into our lives. What He has done in my life, He can and will do in yours. God is not a respecter of persons; we are all equal in His eyes. God has no favorites; rather, we are all His favorites.

My husband and I have three amazing, grown, daughters and I love and cherish each one separately and uniquely because of who they are. Each one of them is distinctly different from the others and I love each one as a special, matchless, gift of life. I truly believe this is how our heavenly Father sees each one of us, as His children, unique, special and full of so much potential.

Around the year 2011, I began working with an organization that ministered to teen girls who had been rescued from human sex trafficking. The two and half years I spent living amongst them and taking care of them, changed me immensely. I saw shame on a completely new level working with these girls and it broke my heart.

In my work with survivors of sex trafficking, I began to clearly see the dire effects of deep, penetrating, shame. I quickly realized how shame has the power to shape and mold our core identity.

This statement was from an email I received just last year:

> "I was a victim of sexual trafficking as a child and sold when I was a small child and under the influence of the person who bought me for many

years even into adulthood. I have been fighting to be free for the past 10 years, and finally 5 years ago, I began slowly healing in all these areas you talk about. Shame is always the last to be healed because I feel it hides under so many other things. It ultimately keeps the person from establishing relationship with the heavenly father."

On some level, everyone has the potential for shame to be functioning in their life. Most people either don't recognize it or they believe they are powerless to do anything about it.

The good news is there is HOPE! As you read this book, I pray that the ugly face of shame will be fully uncovered and you will be able to recognize it operating in your own life.

> ... **"*instead of your shame, I will give you double honor*"**... *(Isaiah 61:7 NKJV)*

Journal

Shades of Shame
All He has are broken people

2

Shame is not worrying over what others think or feeling badly for something you have done. Shame runs deeper. It is the internal belief that you are flawed; that *who* you are, at your core, is the problem.

Let's look at the difference between guilt, embarrassment and shame.

> <u>Guilt</u> is an emotion experienced over an action or lack of action; the feeling that "I did something bad."
>
> <u>Embarrassment</u> is a response to something which threatens the image that we project into the world.
>
> <u>Shame</u> is a painful feeling of humiliation or distress caused by the consciousness of wrong behavior. It is the feeling that "I am bad."

The strongholds of shame are like cords that wrap around an individual keeping them bound in layers of shame.

When someone does not understand the concept of shame and how it could be operating in their life, it will be very difficult to minister to them or help them walk out of a destructive behavior pattern.

Matchbox Twenty said it well in the song 'Back 2 Good'.
> "...well everyone here hides shades of shame,
> Yeah but looking inside we're the same
> We're the same and we're all grown now
> Yeah, but we don't know how
> To get it back to good..."

Whether your shame comes from your own actions, or things that were done to you, or from lies you were told about yourself, trust that God makes beauty out of the messes that people make, when we turn them over to Him.

With all you have to be ashamed of, why would God want you? Love you? Simply put, all He has are broken people. God doesn't see your shame. He sees your growth, your future and your heart. He sees all the potential you have and has plans and dreams for you, far beyond anything you could imagine.

It has been said that breaking up is hard to do. As you work toward dumping shame to move on to greener pastures, you don't have to do it alone. He walks through it with you.

Shame is highly correlated with aggression, depression, suicide, bullying and eating disorders and other addictions. This chaos and discomfort are not in God's plan for your life. So go ahead, break up with shame...you're not married to it!

Dear Shame,

Let's break up! We have been in this toxic relationship for far too long. You are cruel and dishonest.

You smother me, never leaving me with just a few moments to myself. I can't believe I ever listened to your negativity and lies.

Every day with you was complete misery. I've finally realized that I am worthy of love and respect and I have to let you go.

I know that I'll see you again in the future and when I do, I won't be afraid to look you in the face. I'll just never let you back into a position where you can control my life.

Goodbye shame.

Journal

Coming Out of Your Wilderness

A look back at shame in biblical times

"Who is this coming up out of the wilderness, leaning upon her beloved?" (Song of Solomon 8:5 NIV)

I remember the exact moment when I had my epiphany. I can recall the emotion I felt when I saw there was an invitation being extended to me which would enable me to start walking out of my wilderness of depression, pain and shame.

One day I was reading in the Song of Solomon, chapter 2, where we find the Beloved speaking to His lover, a Shulamite woman.

"My beloved said to me, 'Rise up, my love, my fair one, and come away. For the winter is past, the rain is over and gone. The flowers are springing up and the time of the singing of birds has come. Yes, spring is here. The leaves are coming out, and the grapevines are in blossom. How delicious they smell! Arise, my love, my fair one, and come away." (Song of Sol. 2:10-13 TLB)

I could actually hear the Lord speaking to me, at that moment at my kitchen table, to rise up and come away with Him. I sensed that He wanted to draw me aside and away, so that He could minister to me. Unfortunately, I had no idea how to do that.

However, as I stayed with the Lord and continued reading His precious Word, I began to see a pattern of how our Lord relates with people who are carrying things they were never designed to hold.

I want to take you on a journey into the life of someone in scripture- the woman caught in adultery. Over the years, as I have read her story, I would often sit and ponder who she must have been. We only get a snap shot of her life from John 8:3-11, but something inside of me kept causing me to imagine her life and what it must have been like before she encounters the man, Jesus.

I actually felt God's spirit asking me to bring this woman to life in a way that we could relate to her situation and pain. To personalize her in a dimension that would enable us to understand the true cycle and depth of pain and shame.

I only ask that you read with an open heart of compassion and ask the Lord what He would have you glean from her story.

Her name is Shedara, from the Hebrew word Shedar, which means *to struggle and/or to strive*. My prayer is that you will be able to connect with her life as you see her struggle and strive to grab a hold of peace, joy and identity.

Another illusive dream had kept Shedara from getting a good night's rest. She wondered if she would ever be free from the memories that haunted her–memories that kept her tied to her past; a past that she desperately wanted to escape.

Falling into a worn chair, she prepared her breakfast of bread and molded cheese. As she tore at the flat bread in front of her, she gazed through her open door. The dwellings of the lower part of Jerusalem, where she lived, were modest. Houses were stacked tightly together, built with stone that was found in abundance. With no family to help her, Shedara lived in poverty. However, Shedara was grateful. It was the only inheritance she would receive. Everything else had been sold to pay off her mother's hungry creditors.

Suddenly, something caught her eye. She squinted past the door. Who was that approaching? It looked like Daniel darting through her neighbor's courtyard?

"He's out particularly early." Shedara thought. Before she could form another thought, Daniel rushed into her home and slammed the door. Neither one spoke as they looked into each other's eyes. Daniel's dark, wavy hair was messy and his black eyes smoldered. His chest heaved rapidly from running. She knew what he wanted. The same thing all men wanted who came to her house; paid pleasure from her. And in return, she collected a few mites; the smallest value of Hebrew currency.

Although Daniel was a married man, he still wandered outside his marriage bed to fulfill his lustful desires.

Something Shedara was sure that Daniel's wife knew nothing about.

She began to open her mouth and protest but remembered her money pouch had been void of copper coins for many days. Slowly, she nodded her head and began to walk toward the tattered quilts lying on her floor.

Something did not seem right. Daniel had never come to her this early in the morning. Usually he stole to her house under the cover of darkness. To come boldly during daylight seemed peculiar. With growing doubt, she stopped and turned around.

Quickly, Daniel put his hand over her mouth, grabbed her arm and threw her to the ground. Before she could react, he ripped her tunic from her body. She struggled and kicked. Her thoughts were racing. Fear, panic, and helplessness engulfed her. Daniel had never used such force before. Why was he acting so cruelly?

Shedara realized it was useless to fight. She lay still and allowed him to have his way. His heavy body smothered her. Warm tears streamed down her face and his stale breath assaulted her.

Jerking her head back he hissed, "Admit it Shedara, you know I am your favorite." She closed her eyes and hated herself. Moments like this were a brutal reminder of the vow she had made upon her mother's death bed. A promise that she would never participate in the shameful acts her mother had enjoyed. But her destiny was sealed; the generational iniquity passed down from her mother would continue and she felt powerless to stop its vicious cycle.

Suddenly, Shedara's wooden door burst open and a mob of angry men barged into her home. She recognized one of the men as being one of the chief Pharisees along with several Temple scribes. They held such disdain for her in their dark eyes. What were they doing here? And how did they know where she lived?

Daniel jumped off of her quickly and straightened his robe. He looked at one of the Pharisee's with a strange smile on his face. Not saying a word, he ducked his head and quickly left. The group of men simply parted, allowing him to pass through.

Embarrassed and confused, Shedara pulled her torn tunic over her in a vain attempt to hide her nakedness.

One of the older scribes came and stood over her with a triumphant smile. "Pick her up!" He shouted at the temple guards who stood outside her door. Two of the men ran forward and pulled her to her feet.

Her eyes brimmed with dismay. Squeezing them tight, she fought back the hot tears. She refused to give them the pleasure of seeing her cry. She knew the consequences to her actions. She knew what the law demanded of her crime. Yet, time after time Shedara ignored this and continued her desperate search for someone's acceptance. It was this search for unconditional love that drove her again and again into the arms of lusty and unbridled men. The deep void Shedara felt inside her belly would always draw her back, like a cold magnet, back into her own filthy vomit.

"Maybe this time it will be different." She would try to convince herself. "Maybe this time he will stay." "Perhaps this man will truly love me, need me, and find value in me."

The familiar mocking echoed in her head, "No one will ever love you Shedara. The love you seek is only a fantasy. You have no worth. Things will never be different."

Angry guards shouted at her and pushed her towards the door. One of the men threw a tattered shawl over her face. "Cover yourself, harlot woman!" He spat at her as his fist landed a harsh blow to her face.

The soldiers laughed and kicked at her as they shoved her towards the door. She dropped her head and allowed herself to be dragged out into the dusty street. Pride rose up within her and she felt herself try to resist, but she knew it was hopeless. She yielded herself and allowed the angry guards to carry her away like the strong tide of the sea.

She instinctively knew they were taking her up to the Temple Mount, into the courtyard. It was the most sacred site in all of Jerusalem. She knew the high priest would be her judge. He would determine her fate based on the law given by God through Moses.

The Palestinian sun was sweltering and the Temple area was thronged with people. Many gathered daily to hear the teachings of the sages and rabbis. It was unusually quiet this morning. There was only one voice that could be *heard; a voice that held great authority. Everyone was intently listening to a young rabbi speak. Shedara could hear his gentle yet convicting words as the guards dragged her deliberately up the stone steps.*

She felt like she was moving in slow motion. The mob of men that held her captive was arguing loudly among themselves. She heard Daniel's name repeated. Where had he disappeared? She knew that both of them should appear before the high priest. He was just as guilty as she was. Shedara probed the crowd looking for her partner in crime.

As the temple guards rushed to see what was causing the commotion, her accusers threw her at the feet of the rabbi. There was complete silence. Kneeling before him, she knew that she should not dare to look up into his face, yet she could not help herself. This man had such a presence of gentleness about him that she had never encountered before.

Slowly, she lifted her head. As her gaze caught his, she could see her own face reflected back through his hazel eyes. Her image revealed traces of dried blood around her eyes. She winced as she noticed the numerous cuts and bruises upon her face from her accusers. She began to shake uncontrollably.

One of the Pharisees spoke loudly. "This woman was caught in adultery, in the very act. The law of Moses demands stoning. What do you say?" The Pharisee had an evil, smug, look on his face, almost as if every single one of his words held a special bait to trap them all.

Shedara was locked into the young rabbi's stare. It was mesmerizing. Suddenly she never wanted to leave his eyes, for they seemed to drip with liquid love. The young rabbi continued to search her face, as if he could see deep inside her, into the very core of her being. His expression held no trace of condemnation or judgments. Only streams of mercy radiating from him.

Suddenly, she felt the internal cords that held her bound begin to loosen their grip. It was almost as if someone opened the cage door that was holding her captive, giving her permission to fly. Her body began to shake violently. What was happening to her? Why was she shaking so profusely?

As she peered at the faces of those crowded around her, confusion filled her mind. She gazed upon faces filled with pity and fear and yet others were full of self-righteousness and anger.

Calmly the rabbi stooped to the ground and began to write something into the sand as if he had not heard the accusation. Shedara was completely bewildered. Not a sound was made among all of the spectators until, finally, a Pharisee dared to break the silence.

He stood proudly with his hands held clenched. Raising them up into the air, he yelled louder. "I tell you again, this woman is a harlot. She was caught in the very act of adultery. We demand punishment according to our law!"

The crowd turned to see the rabbi's response, waiting and wondering. However, the voice that answered them was calm and gentle, "Whoever is without sin, pick up a stone and throw it first". The rabbi then stooped over and continued to etch his writing into the dry, Judean sand. Shedara did not understand that the strong hand that was etching words into the dusty sand of Jerusalem was also the same hand that had given Moses their commandments for life. Little did she know that she was about to have an encounter with so much grace and mercy that it would change her destiny forever!

Shedara felt herself stiffen. As a young girl, she had been a witness at several public stonings. Never would she forget the cries of anguish and pain from the victim. It was a slow and terrifying death as the stones would be hurled over and over until no one could see the body. Was this her fate? Is this how she would finish out her last breath?

Her enemies were too big for her now. She must rest in what was destined to follow. As she closed her eyes and braced herself for the first blow, she heard the scuffling of footsteps. She looked up and saw that the men were beginning to walk away. Shaking their heads and whispering underneath their breath, each one turned and left. Shedara was amazed and stunned!

Quickly, she turned her head towards the young rabbi before her. She searched his face for the answers to her many questions.

He spoke softly, "Where are your accusers, woman? Is there anyone to condemn you?"

Gazing around her, she could see they were all alone. She

reached out for the strong arm offered to her and stood to her feet. With barely a whisper she breathed. "There is no one, Master."

There was a long pause and then the rabbi's voice answered her. "Then neither do I condemn you; go and sin no more."

Shedara's empty soul filled with a new emotion, something called hope. Never experiencing this sensation before, she felt giddy.

At once she remembered the familiar words of the ancient writings– promises spoken by their beloved King David, "The great One brings them out of the darkness and the shadow of death. He breaks their chains into pieces." These were scriptures her mother had quoted to her as a little girl. Her head filled with doubt. No. This man could not be the one, could he?

Astonished, she remained fixed where she stood. The deep love that permeated out of the man before her was intoxicating. Feeling light and a little dizzy, she closed her eyes and stumbled forward.

A slow smile spread across the face of the young rabbi, called Jesus. Profound joy and peace were present. Peace that Shedara thought was unattainable in this life. Who was this man standing in front of her, reaching for her with such tenderness?

Jesus reached out and stroked the bruise on her face. He lovingly wiped away the dried blood above her brow. His compassion was undeniable and yet confusing. Why did this holy man touch her? Did he not understand who she was? The warmth of his hand stayed on her cheek even after he removed it. Raising his right arm in a gesture of release, he whispered, "Go in peace."

She held her breath. Slowly, she began to back her way down the temple steps. Thoughts raced through her mind as she reached the bottom stair. What just happened? The entire incident only lasted a few minutes, but time seemed to stand still. She could not believe what had transpired. One minute she was facing death and the next moment ... life.

Gazing up into the clear sky of her homeland she saw a lone eagle soaring majestically. Musing on all that had taken place, she hugged herself tightly. Who was this peculiar man? What was his name? Her mind repeated all the events that had taken place in the last hour. This man certainly commanded the Pharisees respect and left everyone puzzled. Why was she thrown at his feet? And why did the Pharisee ask him to pass judgment on her transgression? The more she thought about all that occurred, more questions arose inside of her.

Running home she knew she must find the answers. Where does this man stay? Who are his friends? Could he be the One the prophets said would come? This question stopped her in her tracks.

That evening, laying on the cold, dirt floor of her home, she pondered all the details of the day. What were the words the rabbi spoke as he released her? "Go in Peace?" Peace *was something Shedara had chased all of her life but, could never seem to attain.*

Perhaps Shedara's mother was a single woman who sold herself to men in order to have money to live. Shedara's life would have been filled with what the bible calls *generational iniquity*. This is a gross injustice or wickedness that is passed down from one generation to the next. I imagine that Shedara grew up watching her mother's life and despised it, but found herself doing the very same thing that she loathed about her mother….selling her soul in order to survive.

There is not one, single, little girl who grows up dreaming of the day when she will become a prostitute or an adulterer. It happens over time and most often as a result of circumstances in their life where they believe they don't have any other choice but to engage in this behavior.

I don't know if you can relate to this story, but I sure can. I allowed my own life to become something of promiscuity and defilement in order to believe someone loved me or approved of me. I hated myself for the things I did. Like Shedara, I was thrown into the face of Christ and when I saw my reflection staring back at me through His eyes of grace – it changed me.

If Shedara were alive today, I believe we could become very good friends. In the short encounter she had with Jesus of Nazareth, her entire life changed. Jesus did not judge or condemn her. He dealt with her in a very merciful way. He covered her sin instead of exposing it and this is what transformed her life. I imagine that if we were to interview her immediately afterwards, her head would still be reeling with the feeling of intoxicating love. I believe that, like this woman, our lives can be radically transformed by receiving the fullness of Christ's love. His love truly changes everything.

Though we know nothing of this woman's life after her brief encounter with Jesus, I am convinced she left the steep, stone, steps of the temple that day a different person. I know this because you cannot encounter the grace and mercy of the Father, through the person of Jesus, and not be changed.

It is my hope and prayer that as you read this book that you, too, will be cast onto the truths of Christ and that it will bring a lasting change and freedom into your life.

Journal

Make Pain Your Friend   4
Shine light on the darkness

"Be strong and of good courage; do not be afraid, nor be dismayed, for the LORD your God is with you wherever you go." (Joshua 1:9 NKJV)

There is more to Shedara's story, but I leave that to you to finish. However, I am convinced that as she experienced her deliverer, up close and personal, she received His grace and love, and therefore was finally able to walk out of her wasteland of shame and self-loathing. I believe this, because it happened to me and I know it is possible.

I can relate to Shedara's life in more ways than one. I, too, struggled to find a life of purpose, identity and peace for many years. My own story is one filled with brokenness, abandonment, sexual abuse and rejection. However, even though telling my story and inviting the Lord into those places of deep pain and rejection were some of the hardest things I have ever done, it was vitally necessary in order to capture what I so desperately needed- true identity, joy and finally, PEACE!

As a small child, all I wanted was my daddy's approval and acceptance. I remember being mesmerized by him as a small girl and always wanting to spend time with him. He was a successful business man who seemed continuously busy. Dressed spotlessly and in the latest fashion of the day, my dad was handsome and strong. I believed him to be invincible. I think back to those days and all I wanted was for him to notice me.

Though I desperately sought my earthly father's love, what I really needed was to understand and know the love of the One who created and formed me. It wasn't until I reached my 20s that the beginning of this reality came to me. It has taken me almost 30 years to fully grasp and understand that the kind of love given by God, through Jesus, was the love I had been seeking all along.

I grew up singing the old, familiar, song, "Jesus loves me, this I know, for the bible tells me so..." However, these were just happy words that didn't really have the power to fill the deep void that was inside of me.

As human beings we are created to bond with our Creator and to others. Whether you like it or not, you were created dependent and needy. We all have needs, and those needs must be met. However, we must ultimately turn to the One who has placed that neediness in us for fulfillment. Our problems occur when we attempt to get our needs met in ways other than those within the boundaries created by God. The need to bond and attach with others is woven deep in our DNA.

I believe the heavy cloak of shame is the chief robber of true intimacy. We all want intimacy and connection in our relationships – it is what we were created for.

In my work with survivors of sexual abuse and torment, I heard repeatedly the fact that they believed they were damaged or defective on many levels. I remember one sweet teenage girl had literally carved, into her leg, the words, "*I deserve to die.*" Her belief that she was deeply flawed led her to the conclusion that death was the only escape from her torment. The intense belief of shame can be consuming and excruciating because there seems to be no hope in reversing its condition. In my humble opinion, it is the worst feeling ever experienced by mankind.

When someone is walking in deep shame, it becomes a wall that separates them from others. The very people whom you desire a connection with are the ones that are blocked access to your true self. The primary goal of a shame-led person is to stay safe, and to self-protect.

Have you ever tried to develop a relationship with someone and it was going really well and then "a wall went up" and you could feel the person moving away from you? It is very difficult to develop true intimacy in any relationship when one is always trying "to be safe."

I believe abandonment and rejection play a huge part in building the foundation on which shame sits. The pain that comes with abandonment or rejection is something we don't want to keep experiencing, so we push it down and hide it, from ourselves and others.

The cries of our soul from the pain that we are experiencing, may often reveal deep and hidden wounds. They expose the sorrows of our own life – things that have happened to us or things that we have engaged in either unintentionally or voluntarily. Deeper still, they reveal how our heart is connecting with God.

Pain will always pursue pleasure. But if you will stay with me, I promise I will help you de-mystify the idea that pain is your enemy and like me, you can actually learn to embrace it. A good friend of mine always says, "Put pain get on the payroll?" In other words, make pain give you a good pay back!

Through the Psalms, God shows us how to engage with Him in our struggles. As we participate in this way we are able to see His perception of things. Through this we can learn and grow. God created our emotions and He wants us to acknowledge and experience them. In doing this, we learn what true intimacy is supposed to look like as we partake of God and share with Him our deepest thoughts and emotions. Only then can we allow Him to untangle everything that is going on inside of us.

When we come to God in prayer and supplication, we empty out a part of us. Today, you can empty out a part of yourself that is holding pain, heartache, hurt, grief and agony. As you pour out the pain in your heart to God, He refills your inner being with more of Himself. God is love and there is great healing within Him. (Psalm 103:1-5; 1 John 4:16)

This is what I call the "sacred trade." You give God all of your pain and He heals you and refills your heart with His purpose and plans. Sometimes our pain is taking up so much space that it is difficult to find God's destiny inside. Will you pray this prayer with me today?

> Dear heavenly Father, I surrender to you all of my pain, it is too much for me to carry. I need your comfort and guidance while I look for ways that I can grow in all of this. I know you have a good and perfect plan for my life and I trust you to open my eyes so that I can see what you see. I know you work all things together for my good and for Your glory. I put on your strength in order to move past my pain. I ask you teach me how to walk with you daily, moment by moment.

You may experience anger surfacing as you start discovering the lies of shame in your life. This is common and certainly understandable. Please do not run from the pain you may be feeling. The clutches of shame that are chocking the life and vitality from you can be broken. I promise you can find healing when you walk through the pain, not by avoiding it. We learn best when we go through the struggle and not around it.

As we understand that at the very core of our shame, we have lost our dignity, we can begin to ask our heavenly Father to reassemble the pieces of our identity.

The origin of the word dignity is 'worthy.' Meanings include 'worthy of honor or respect' and 'a sense of pride in oneself or self respect.'

I believe that true healing and restoration occurs when we courageously step into our stories of pain and harm. We are then enabled and empowered to share it with others. I believe everyone has a story to tell; even our heavenly Father had a story – one He has shared with the whole world. A story filled with pain, brokenness and evil. Yet out of that story came hope, strength and restoration that is available for all!

As we begin to share our pain and emotions with others, something very organic and powerful happens. We find comfort in knowing that we are not the only one that has been shattered by the evils of this world. We begin to find "shalom - peace, harmony, wholeness, completeness, prosperity, welfare and tranquility" in every dimension of our lives.

I have learned, in telling my story, that my emotions rise to the surface, but this needs to happen in order for a loving Father to bring healing. This requires the courage to break through my fears of someone else knowing my weaknesses and failures. When I am brave enough to share my story with others, it creates a sense of safety, a community that is authentic and real and allows me to be fully known. In my experience with groups of people that are recovering from the effects of shame, you can visibly see a profound difference in them as they begin to share their story with others.

What is the cost involved for you to open up and bare your soul? Only you can answer that question. But I can tell you that when you venture out and embrace the fullness of who you are - it will empower you to be an agent of transformation in the lives of others.

Allow the Holy Spirit to talk with you regarding your emotions. He will speak and show you things about yourself you did not know. Some things you may have tried burying in the recesses of the dark because they feel too painful, but God wants all things to come to His marvelous light. Trust Him to bring you out and into His love and power of healing.

 Look up Psalms 139:23 and write it out:

> *".....The Lord will bring to light the hidden things of darkness and reveal the counsels of the heart."* (I Corinthians 4:5 NKJV)

What does God say He will bring to the light?

In John 10:3-5, Jesus said His followers would hear His voice and another voice they would not follow.

If you belong to Him, you have the ability to hear Him speak to you. Jesus said, **"My sheep hear my voice and I know them…."** *(John 10:27 NJKV)*

This is one of the greatest gifts that God has given us – the ability to communicate with Him. This is not necessarily an audible voice that you hear with your physical ear, but a knowing inside of your being, that God is communicating His heart to you.

When the Holy Spirit speaks to you He creates the message inside of your heart. In one moment, there may be nothing and in the next instant His message will exist inside of your spirit. You most likely will not hear, see, feel, taste or smell anything because God rarely communicates through our physical senses. It will simply be a "knowing" that is within you and your heart will have peace.

> *"You will keep him in perfect peace, whose mind is stayed on You, because He trusts in You."* (Isaiah 26:3 NKJV)

I encourage you to begin posturing yourself daily to commune with Him. This will mean you may have to find a quiet place, and block out all distractions. As you do, you will clearly be able to distinguish His sound from all others. God speaks to us through His Word, primarily, and He certainly uses other people to speak to us, sometimes even angels. However, I truly believe His preference is to speak to us directly - His Spirit to our heart.

Close your eyes and be still and ask your heavenly Father if there is anything that may be hiding in the darkness. List anything that comes to your mind.

The good news is that Jesus came to heal the broken hearted.

"The spirit of the LORD God is upon Me, because the LORD has anointed Me to preach good tiding to the poor; He has sent Me to heal the brokenhearted, to proclaim liberty to the captives, and the opening of the prison to those who are bound." (Isaiah 61:1NKJV)

The entire chapter of Isaiah 61 is the directive that the Father gave the Son for all of mankind. God knew our hearts would be bruised and battered and for some even broken into many pieces. However, the good news is that Jesus has the power and is willing to bring healing to every part of our heart that we give to Him. Do not be afraid! The Father takes great joy in restoring every part of your soul that has been crushed by the traumas of this world.

Journal

Identity Theft 5
Feelings and behavior are not who we really are

"You took away my worth!"

The headlines screamed at me and caused me to slow down and do a double take. I am sure most of us have heard or read about the story of the sexual assault of the unconscious young lady by a male Stanford student. The story has caused outrage and division among people as to what is fair and just punishment. What I find so disturbing from this entire event is the fact that the young lady who was assaulted now believes she has no worth….no value…no voice.

The demeaning assault made against her has formed a dark shroud of shame over her. "Emily Doe" has now become intimately acquainted with dishonor, humiliation and mortification. By her own words, she emphatically states, "the damage is done, and no one can undo it."

As I mentioned earlier, shame is the belief that one is uniquely and fatally flawed. Most people do not understand the difference between shame and guilt. Shame comes from who we are and guilt is what we feel when we do something wrong. Traumatic events, molestation, sexual defilement of all kinds, rape, and abandonment are all things which can cause shame to come upon a person. The younger the person is when experiencing shame the more devastating it can be.

In the inner dialogue from a shaming event, "Why?" is always the question.

- Why is my grandfather doing this to me?
- What is the matter with me?
- Why am I different?
- Why am I not able to obtain freedom from some of the things in my life that are wrong?

With questions like that, the answers often look like this:

- I must be uniquely and fatally flawed.
- I must be the only person like this.
- No one understands me.
- I am powerless.

To believe one is hopelessly flawed means "there is nothing I can do about it." "I am so bad or so wounded that even God cannot help me." This belief system can spiral downward quickly and cause people to isolate themselves from the very people who can help them heal from their hidden wounds.

I believe shame is a tool forged by the hand of our greatest adversary, Satan. With it, he wields blows against our self-worth and knocks us down to levels that seem nearly impossible to rise up from. Shame then becomes a barrier that has the perceived power to prevent us from experiencing the love and destiny that God has designed for us.

Shameful events can and do happen to all of us – some are mild like bullying or name-calling, but others are deeply distressing and crippling. They typically come into our lives uninvited, or as a result of some very poor choices. It is what we do with the events, themselves, that determines if and how we overcome them. The good news is there is someone who can "undo shame." The harrowing and painful deeds of the past CAN be remedied.

I have counseled and ministered to many young girls and women who have been sexually abused, hurt and molested. All of them have come away with a sense that their inward self is hopelessly flawed; that something is intrinsically wrong with them. All the therapy of the modern day will not be able to permeate the layers of shame and allow the healing process to begin if they don't turn to the One who created them. The healing process requires us to recognize that our identity is tied to who we are in Christ. The events of the past, although hurtful and part of our life experiences, do not define who we are.

> *"We're going to have to let truth scream louder to our souls than the lies that have infected us."*
> ~Beth Moore

True restoration results from being molded by the Word within, rather than the world without. It starts with believing God's truths and knowing He is the One who has the power to bring lasting deliverance and healing.

 Read and circle where our help comes from.

"I will lift up my eyes to the hill, from where comes my help? My help comes from the LORD, Who made heaven and earth." (Psalm 121:1 NKJV)

The Creator of the Universe is our helper. He knows us better than anyone and understands our pain. Psalms 139 tells us that God formed us and shaped us in our mother's wombs.

 Read Psalm 139:13-15 and write out what you discover.

In verse 16 of this same Psalm, David writes, "Your eyes saw my substance, being yet unformed. And in Your book they all were written, the days fashioned for me; when as yet there were none of them."

You may have gone through some extremely traumatic experiences that have stolen your dignity and self worth. If you are willing to bring your pain to the throne of Jesus, even if you have to drag it there kicking and screaming, He can and will heal and restore every dirty and hurtful event in your life.

Read Isaiah 61:7 below and underline the promises made by God.

> *"Instead of your shame you shall have double honor and instead of confusion they shall rejoice in their portion. Therefore in their land they shall possess double; Everlasting joy shall be theirs."* (Isaiah 61:7 NKJV)

God promises that for every ounce of shame you have encountered, He has a double portion of honor to bestow upon you. Thank Him, today, for this promise and make this a part of your daily declaration as you walk through your journey of healing.

God can, and will, use those destructive circumstances that have happened to work out for our good. When we give God the pieces of our brokenness and allow Him to hold them in His hand, He will shape them into a beautiful piece of art.

> *"And we know that all things work together for good to those who love God, to those who are the called according to His purpose."*
> (Romans 8:28 NKJV)

Those events that happened in your life can be turned around and then used to make you into a stronger and better person. When we start looking at our past through the lens of God's perspective, we begin to realize that He did not desire or plan for the hurtful things to happen to us. He has given us His power and grace which will enable us to walk through with our head held high and if we focus on Him. It is in these times that we are given the opportunity to allow His character and nature to be molded within us.

In Ephesians 2:10 the apostle Paul states that we are God's workmanship created, shaped and formed into the likeness of Christ. Our journey with the Lord is just that...a journey. Along the way, He shapes us, each day, more into the beautiful image of His Son.

The word workmanship in Greek is the word *poiema*, which is where we get the English word *poem*. The idea is that God is the master artist and we are His canvas, His work of art. This is how He sees us.

Mankind is the pinnacle of God's creation – above all. When God created man and woman, He stepped back and said "this is good." When we choose to see ourselves the way our heavenly Father sees us, we can have the confidence to be successful in whatever we put our hand to.

As humans, we were not created to endure pain. Our creator had a specific purpose for mankind to enjoy an existence of intense joy and fellowship with Him. He placed Adam and Eve into a beautiful garden of sublime existence where there was no pain or sorrow.

It was only when rebellion and disobedience entered the garden through Adam and Eve's choices, did a profound separation occur. Sadly, this led them to place where they were vulnerable to unseen forces that wanted to steal their true identity.

Bad experiences or painful pasts can negatively affect our present. There are forces of darkness that want us to believe that we are the only ones who suffer with these issues and that it is unchangeable. This is simply not true. Too often our sin and emotional baggage gets linked to what we believe about ourselves. In other words, our personality and identity becomes associated with the things we struggle with.

The strategy of the enemy is for us to believe that we actually "are" how we feel or behave, which is not true at all. Satan wants you to believe things like: you "are" depressed, unhappy, worthless, unable to change, stupid, a failure...the list could go on and on. It is important to realize that our feelings and behavior are situational and we can change them. **The truth is *feelings and behavior are not who we really are*.** They might be things that we struggle with, but they are not our identity, or who we are in Christ.

Your feelings and behavior may be based on how you think about yourself on a deep level. You might not consciously believe these thoughts, but you may find yourself thinking them or saying them about yourself on a regular basis. Most people don't see that there is a direct connection between the way they view themselves and their destiny.

 Look up Proverbs 23:7 and write it out.

Satan wants to steal our identities and take away any hope for change. When he is able to get us to believe his lies about ourselves, he may use Bible truths out of context to release a deadly attack against our destiny.

To experience a radically transformed life we must have a renewed thinking.

The process of renewing your mind involves a principle called *dying to self*. I have always struggled with this concept. Recently, I have begun seeing things in an entirely new light. Renewing my mind looks like this: I find a truth inside of God's Word; I read it, come into agreement with it and then meditate on it. In the book of Colossians, Paul speaks a lot about identity, though sometimes we may not be fully aware of it. In chapter One, Paul is telling the early believers that they had once been alienated or separated from God and that <u>our mind</u> was our own enemy. He goes on to say that NOW we are reconciled or brought back to God in relationship, because the body and blood of Christ has presented us as holy, blameless and above reproach in God's eyes.

Read Colossians 1:21 and 22 and write down what you find.

As I have come into agreement with this truth about how God sees me, I can actually feel the cords of shame begin to loosen around me. God is patiently waiting for all of us to discover who He is so that we can uncover our own true self. Our life is hidden in God because of Christ. (Colossians 3:3) What does that look like to you?

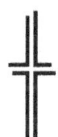

If my life is hidden in God, then who I truly am looks like God Himself. The fruit of God's spirit, or essence, is love, joy, peace, patience, kindness, goodness, and self-control. As we allow our life to be wrapped up inside of the life of Christ, we begin to exhibit these fruits as well. Peace is available today, joy is available, and love and kindness can be found within us.

There are several verses in the Bible that talk about dying to the sinful nature or "old self" and allowing God to live through us. This is a necessary process for transforming your life.

"But put on the Lord Jesus Christ, and make no provision for the flesh, to fulfill its lusts."
(Romans 13:14 NKJV)

In the book of Colossians, Paul urges Jesus' followers to "put on love" above all other things and even calls it the bond of perfection.

Make a list of ways that you can practically "put on" the Lord, Jesus Christ, daily.

We need to be certain of the fact that God has nothing but good intentions for us, even though we may not know or see them yet.

Look up and write out Jeremiah 29:11.

God sees us as who we are becoming, through His love and power. As He looks at our lives, He knows our past, understands our present, and can see us in the future, all at the same time. His love, mercy, and grace are unfathomable. Imagine the possibilities if we could see ourselves the same way that God sees us.

"As a father has compassion on his children, so the LORD has compassion on those who fear him; for He knows how we are formed, and he remembers that we are dust."

(Psalm 103:13-14 NIV)

Our heavenly Father takes into consideration our humanity. His heart breaks for the things that break ours. He is not an angry Father withholding His love and mercy. Remember how Jesus dealt with the woman caught in adultery. He covered her, just like He covered Adam and Even in the beginning when they hid because of their shame. Only they tried to cover themselves with their own efforts. Yet, God stepped in and demonstrated how He covers our sin and shame– by slaying an innocent one and covering our transgressions with sacred blood.

Look up Hebrews 9:12-15. Note verse 14: *"Jesus' blood cleanses our conscience from "dead works."*

These dead works are the activities we involve ourselves in when trying to cover or deal with our own shame. For me, it involved being harder on myself than on anyone else. I would let other people off the hook for things done wrong, but I would beat myself up continually over a failure or mistake I committed. I somehow believed it was my responsibility to punish myself for all the wrong things I did. It was only then that I could believe I was good enough to approach God.

Write out any dead works that you may be engaging in.

One day, I was listening to a preacher who challenged us to declare over ourselves that Jesus Christ was our righteousness. We were to do this many times a day for 30 days, and see what a difference it makes. This truth is found in the New Testament, the book of 2 Corinthians. The apostle Paul is telling the church at Corinth a revolutionary thought. Paul was telling believers that there was nothing they could do in their own strength that could cause them to be in right standing with God.

"For God made Christ, who never sinned, to be the offering for our sin, so that we could be made right with God through Christ."
(2 Corinthians NLT)

There is nothing we can add to the blood of Jesus that will cause God to love or forgive us more. It is done! Jesus declared when He hung on the cross, "It is finished!" When we attempt to beat ourselves up or punish ourselves for not doing what we know we are supposed to do, we are telling God that His plan, the shed blood of His precious Son, was not enough. When this truth got deep inside of me, I fell to my knees and repented. When we come to this realization, a weight is lifted and we can experience the joy of our salvation and walk in the freedom that Christ came to give us.

Oftentimes, the only way God's truths can get down deep inside of us, and produce transformation, is when we ponder or meditate on His Word.

One of the very first bible verses I memorized when I began following Jesus was Joshua 1:8. God is giving instructions to young Joshua on how he is to lead the people out of their wilderness and into their promise land. God tells Joshua that he was to meditate on all the words God had spoken, day and night, so that he could be successful and prosper in whatever he did.

I have taken that challenge over the years for myself. God's Word has the ability to change, re-arrange and transform our lives in a powerful and real way when we get it inside of us. If you have been struggling for a long time in understanding who you are and who God is, then I encourage you to read God's Word daily. His truth is the only thing that dismantles the lies that have formed in our minds.

 Look up Hebrews 4:12 and write out what you learn about the Word of God.

In John 16:13, Jesus is telling his followers that when He leaves, the Spirit of Truth will come and when He does, He will lead them into *all truth.*

Write out the truth that you need to hear from the Holy Spirit involving your identity.

Jesus spoke:

> *"If you abide in My word, you are My disciples indeed. And you shall know the truth and the truth shall make you free."*
>
> (John 8:3-32 NKJV)

The key word is 'abide.' In Greek this means to continue, to remain, to dwell or to stand. As we stay present inside of God's truth, we will be set free from the torture of false beliefs, lies and any half-truths that we have believed. His Word, His truth, even sets us free from the falsehoods we are unaware of.

Take time, today, to pray and ask God to show you what lies you believe about yourself and write it down.

Journal

Healing and Forgiveness
Real healing; a walk through the process of forgiveness

"...God has sent me to preach good news to the poor, to heal the heartbroken..."
(Isaiah 61:1 NKJV)

A wise man once said, "When you forgive, you heal. And when you let go, you grow."

Because relationships are so important to God, learning to forgive is a crucial issue. However, healing from shame involves many facets. One of the main components is forgiveness. We cannot expect to move forward with God when we have bitterness and unforgiveness in our heart. Before we talk about forgiveness, I want to take you back to the Old Testament, to the book of Isaiah, chapter 53. The prophet of old is foretelling about the Messiah, Jesus, who is to come.

I have often said that if I was stranded on a deserted island and only able to have one book of the bible, I would choose the writings of Isaiah.

"Surely He has borne our griefs and carried our sorrows...." *(Isaiah 53:4 NKJV)*

In the New Testament, in the book of Matthew, he is recalling a time when many brought to Jesus the sick and demon-possessed. It says that Jesus cast out the spirits and healed all who were sick. Matthew tells us that when Jesus did this, he was fulfilling the ancient prophecy of Isaiah 53:4. Only Matthew quotes this passage in Greek and it reads, *"He Himself took our infirmities and bore our sicknesses."*

As I began to read both of these passages together, I ran to get my Strong's concordance. I love to study words, their means and origins, and so when I read my bible, I often times will look up different words in the Hebrew and Greek in order to get a full picture of what the author is saying.

In the Isaiah passage, the word "griefs" means malady and/or calamity. It comes from another Hebrew word that means "to be rubbed or worn; to be weak, sick or afflicted." God was stating that He knew His people would be worn down with the sins of this world. That they could become weakened and afflicted because of things done to them or as a result of what our own sin does to our body.

The word "sorrows" in the Isaiah passage means anguish – grief, pain or sorrow. The Creator, God of the universe, had a fore knowledge about His own people. He knew that they could fall into anguish, pain and sorrow as a result of living in this fallen world and He had a solution. He was going to send His son, the Messiah, into the world in order to take all these infirmities and sicknesses upon Himself.

My friend, Jesus can heal you of any affliction that has worn you down and rubbed you raw. The shame you may be carrying can be lifted. The pain and sorrow you are experiencing as a result of trauma or sin can be healed. Jesus came to forgive and to heal!

This same prophecy that is stated by the disciple Matthew, in chapter 7, uses the words 'infirmities and sicknesses.' When you look them up in the Greek it becomes even clearer. The word infirmity in the Greek means "feebleness of body or mind; a sickness; disability or malady".

The Father knew we would have infirmities, and He had a plan in place. The heavy burden of shame upon a person can cause deep feebleness of body and mind. Our soul was not designed to carry this load. It eventually leads to sickness and malady. Webster dictionary states that malady means "an ailment or unwholesome and disordered condition."

Wow – isn't that what shame does to us? It causes a disorder in our body and soul; sometimes to the degree where we are not able to function properly. Shame causes us to hang our head down in heaviness and we disconnect from people. But the good news is that the Lord is the lifter of our head. He stoops low and gently lifts our chin and head up in order that we can see properly and connect with Him and others.

I believe and have experienced this wonder. King David knew this as well and he wrote:

> *"But you, LORD, are a shield around me, my glory, the One who lifts my head high."*
> (Psalms 3:3 NIV)

Take some time right now and let these truths wash over you.

Write down how you have experienced grief and sorrow as well as any infirmities and/or sicknesses. Meditate on Jesus healing you of these ailments and imagine Him coming down and lifting your head! You may want to write out a prayer of thanksgiving as well.

I have seen so many people receive instant healing when they forgave those who hurt them. I had to walk through layers of forgiveness of my own abusers. It took time, and I needed to be intentional, but it is possible. Jesus will walk alongside of you as you travel this road, remember, He knows your sorrows and pain. He understands how you have been rubbed and worn down.

Some people need a good counselor to help them in the process. However, if that is not a road you want to choose at this time, I encourage you to get a notebook and make it into your Forgiveness Journal. I had a counselor that helped me with the forgiveness process and got me on a good track so that I could go at it alone with God.

I began to write down all the things that had happened to me and the people that had done them. I went through each episode and event and chose to forgive. Some of them did not deserve it, or so I believed at the time. That is okay. Forgiving others of the wrongs they have committed is for YOU.

I love the quote that several have spoken: "Unforgiveness is like poison that we drink, and then expect the other person to die." Unforgiveness keeps you in bondage - bondage to insecurities and a dysfunctional lifestyle.

It also binds us emotionally to the one that offended us. Forgiveness does not necessarily mean reconciliation. Forgiveness is something you do for yourself. It takes two to reconcile and oftentimes that is not possible in this life. Death may already separate you or prohibit you from reconciling, but you can choose to forgive anyway.

Just because you forgive someone doesn't mean you have to allow them to continue to harm you. Learning good, healthy boundaries will keep you safe and help you move forward.

Forgiveness does not restore trust. Trust must be earned back. This will take time. Forgiveness does not, necessarily, mean there will be reconciliation to a fractured or broken relationship. What it does do is open you, and the other person, up in a way that will allow God's healing, favor and blessings to enter your life.

Another thing I learned was how to erect healthy boundaries in my relationships. This will help you feel empowered and safe while you are healing.

> *"Getting to the next level always requires ending something, leaving it behind, and moving on. Growth demands that we move on. Without the ability to end things, people stay stuck, never becoming who they are meant to be, never accomplishing all that their talents and abilities should afford them."* ~Dr. Henry Cloud

I recommend the book <u>Boundaries: When to Say Yes, How to Say No to Take Control of Your Life</u> by Dr. Henry Cloud and Dr. John Townsend.

When forgiveness replaces bitterness and resentment, a new peace and life will begin to unfold for you. This is a picture of what Christ's forgiveness brings to us.

Forgiveness will set you free – trust me! Use your will and make the decision, that today, you choose to forgive and set yourself free from the prison that holds you bound. Forgiveness is a choice to give up your rights for vengeance, negative thoughts, and bringing consequences upon the offender. Forgiveness will always bring freedom.

Underline what you wish to get rid of and circle what you need God's help with.

"Get rid of all bitterness, rage, anger, harsh words, and slander, as well as all types of evil behavior. Instead, be kind to each other, tenderhearted, forgiving one another, just as God through Christ has forgiven you."
(Ephesians 4:31-32 NLT)

God tells us in His Word that His ways are not our ways, and His thoughts are not our thoughts. God often times will ask us to participate with Him on a matter and it will stretch our own human understanding. But God knows that forgiveness is essential in order to live a peaceful and fruitful life.

Forgiveness is a journey. It most certainly is not a onetime event. Some of the pain you may be experiencing can be very deep. However, I encourage you to make pain your friend and make a decision to walk the path of forgiving those who have hurt you.

We forgive because we make a decision to do so, yet the feeling of forgiveness may come later. You may need to forgive repeatedly, but that is okay. It is also important to understand, forgiving is not about forgetting – we cannot stuff away our hurts. I often say that feelings buried alive never die. They only intensify and grow.

Sometimes, the person we need to forgive the most is ourselves. I know for me, it was easier to forgive those who had hurt me, than to forgive myself of all the things I had done. I realized I had been holding myself hostage by not extending the same degree of forgiveness to myself that I did to others.

I remember the day when my counselor encouraged me to stand in front of a full length mirror, without any clothes covering me and speak out loud to myself all the things I had done wrong. This was one of the most painful things I have had to do in my own healing journey. I had so much self-hatred that it was very difficult for me to look at myself completely exposed. However, I pushed past the negative emotions and did what she asked. Every day it got easier and easier.

I believe we become so comfortable wearing costumes and masks to hide who we truly are, that when we are exposed, our first response is to quickly cover back up. In my mirror exercise I could not meet my own reflection in the mirror. It was very challenging to look myself in the eye and forgive myself. In doing this, we allow our true self to come forward, into the light, where there is love, healing and peace.

If you decide to take this challenge, I encourage you to go slow and be intentional. You may only be able to do this for short periods of time and it may take days and weeks for you to feel comfortable looking at yourself fully. As you stay with it, I believe you will be able to offer forgiveness to yourself.

The reality is that we all mess up, we all make mistakes and have deep regrets over things we have done. A lot of the things we do and the decisions we make come out of the pain of our brokenness and shame.

Do yourself a favor, extend mercy over yourself for all you have done. Jesus died for each and every deed you have committed. His blood is powerful enough to forgive and cleanse. You only need to BELIEVE.

Forgiveness is the essence of love. You are valuable and you deserve to be forgiven and God will empower you with His strength to extend forgiveness to others.

Prayer of Forgiveness

All of us have been hurt by others. Make a quick review of the people in your story. Is there anyone who causes a level of anger or resentment to rise in your heart? While you may feel that holding onto resentment and anger punishes the one who hurt you, the painful truth is it is your heart that is held captive. It is time to set yourself free from the prison of unforgiveness. Forgiving someone does not mean that what they did was okay. Forgiveness is trusting God to be your righteous judge and loving Father.

Dear Father,
I have been hurt and wounded by others. While they were wrong in their actions and words toward me, I have also been wrong in my sinful responses toward them. Your Word says that Jesus was bruised for our transgression, and by His stripes we are healed. Take from me any pain I have been holding onto in regard to this person. I don't want to carry it anymore.

I confess the sin of judging them and their specific offenses against me. Forgive me for the anger and hatred I have had in my heart against them. Thank You for forgiving me through the blood of Jesus.
I choose to forgive and release them of all my judgments. I let go of all bitterness, resentment, and ungodly attitudes. All judgment belongs to you. Where there has been injustice, I choose to let You be Judge, and I trust You to care for me. Your power and grace are at work in me. I receive all Your gracious work in my life and choose to live in tune with Your heart for this person.
In Jesus' name, Amen

Declaration of Release

Now that you have asked God to forgive you, a declaration of release is needed. Release is spoken to the offender, whether they are present or absent, living or dead. It recognizes that our words and actions have bound them and, equally as important, bind us to the offending person. It is very liberating to speak or write this release to them if we can. With God's power it can be done.

> Because Jesus Christ is my Lord, I free everyone from my judgments and sinful responses. I give you back to God the Father, Son, and Holy Spirit. I place you at God's throne of grace. I want my heart to be free. I trust God to work in you and in me, in His time and in His way. I choose to see you as God sees you. I bless you to be all God called you to be. I will continue to ask for God's love for you. I cannot impose my will or expectations upon you, so I place all my expectations on the cross of Jesus. I know that God has good plans and purposes for each of us. I release you. I give you entirely to God. I loose you and let you go. We are both free.

Journal

Purpose and Passion
God delights in you

The fact that God has a purpose for your life is stated throughout scripture.

> *"For I know the plans, or purposes, I have for you, says the Lord. Plans for good and not for evil; to give you a future and a hope."*
> (Jeremiah 29:11 NKJV)

As we read the bible, it shows us that God's plan is for mankind to live with purpose, vision and passion.

As we have looked at how God has dealt with shame within His people, we can clearly see who God is and who He is NOT. We can now begin to form our own identity based on who He is, and not on our past experiences, failures or false beliefs.

Our true self, our identity, is who we are as God's children. He distinctly created us as individuals for our unique place in this world.

Your primary purpose is to know God and receive all of His love. As you do this, you will begin to see your special temperament that God gave you when He first created you. King David wrote, *"For you, Lord, formed my inward parts; you covered me in my mother's womb."* (Psalm 139:13 NKJV)

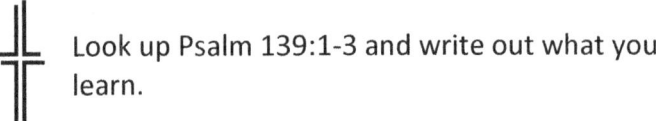 Look up Psalm 139:1-3 and write out what you learn.

Your unique temperament will show up in how you interact in social circles, your personal preferences and how you give and receive affection in your relationships. Some people like to be around a lot of people and are very happy being the center of attention and some prefer silence or only a few people to socialize with. Everyone is different and created by God with a unique blueprint. My prayer is that you will embrace yours and value the differences in others. No two of us are alike. And when shame is completely removed, you may find yourself looking completely different than what you thought or others have told you.

I encourage you to start telling your story. First, in confession to your heavenly Father who loves you like no other; but press on and share it with trusted others who are able to identify your deep woundedness and your deep goodness. As a result, you will increase your capacity to know and live out your calling and engage in life-giving relationships with God and others.

As you look at your own story of shame and adversity, you will begin to understand more about who God is and who He created you to be. As you perceive and understand what the enemy of your life has tried to accomplish in destroying you through shame, you are able to be filled with hope that things can actually change.

Your purpose will always include your passions and your abilities. It will include ALL of your experiences....the good, the bad, and the ugly. God redeems everything.

You and I have a divine design. We were created for God and to live in His kingdom. He has given each of His children a calling and a purpose to fulfill, inside His kingdom. If you belong to God then you have a purpose, and when you discover that then everything changes.

Underline what God works together for your good.

"And we know that God causes everything to work together for the good of those who

love God and are called according to his purpose for them." (Romans 8:28 NLT)

That is right – everything! Whatever God has called you to do or be a part of, He will give you the grace to complete. That is good news.

What may look like a closed door to you could be God's way to a bigger blessing. What appears to be a nightmare can become His dream for your marriage. And what may seem like the worst possible news you could receive can actually be a place of a brand new beginning. This is only possible because whatever God allows to touch your life is part of His plan for your future.

Read the following passage of scripture and underline or circle the most meaningful promise for you.

"You shall also be a crown of glory in the hand of the LORD, and a royal diadem in the hand of your God. You shall no longer be termed Forsaken, nor shall your land anymore be termed Desolate; But you shall be called Hephzibah and your land Beulah; for the LORD delights in you and your land shall be married." (Isaiah 62:3-4 NKJV)

You are the one whom the Lord delights in, my friend. He declares that you are no longer barren with shame or forgotten, but married to Him. In covenant, through Jesus' blood, you have been purchased and given a new identity and purpose. You are now a son or daughter of the Most High God.

As you exchange the false beliefs of who you are for the reality of who God says you are, a great awakening will occur in your soul.

Read the scripture below and underline what you find most important.

"You are of God, little children, and have overcome, because He who is in your is greater than he who is in the world."
(I John 4:4 NKJV)

John goes on to say in this chapter that God is love and the one who abides or stays IN love abides inside of God and God IN him. *(I John 4:16 NKJV)*

All God can love is who you really are, your *true self*, because that is the only thing that exists anyway.

Journal

Finding Satisfaction 8
Allowing your soul to be restored

> *"Until now you have not asked for anything in my name. Ask and you will receive, and your joy will be complete."*
> *(John 16:24 NIV)*

Inside of every human is a cavernous hole that can only be filled by God Himself. The deepest cravings and desires of our soul are meant to be filled with a living, intimate relationship with the One who created us. I am convinced our hearts are not healthy or satisfied until we yield them up to the only perfect love that exists: the love of God Himself.

Since God is love, He embodies the totality of what perfect love looks like. When we position ourselves to encounter this love, our lives are radically transformed. For His love changes everything. There is a powerful invitation extended to mankind from God himself. We find its proclamation in the book of Isaiah. God is speaking and He says:

> *"Ho! Everyone who thirsts,*
> *Come to the waters;*
> *And you who have no money,*
> *Come, buy and eat.*

*Yes, come, buy wine and milk
Without money and without price.
Why do you spend money for what is not bread,
And your wages for what does not satisfy?
Listen carefully to Me, and eat what is good,
And let your soul delight itself in abundance".*
(Isaiah 55:1-2 NKJV)

Our soul is able to delight itself when we partake of the very nature of our heavenly Father.

Read and underline what comes when we trust in the Lord.

"Taste and see that the LORD is good. Oh, the joys of those who take refuge in him!" *(Psalm 34:8NLT)*

I hope you see that joy comes as we taste and put our trust in God. One can experience true joy when their heart is satisfied with knowing God.

As a mother of three daughters, I have realized that the world we live in sends a continual message that, as a woman, your complete satisfaction comes in falling in love with a man and getting married. I think of all the cartoon movies that my girls watched and most of them had a message that happiness came when your prince comes and rescues you out of a bad situation. When our knight in shining armor sweeps us off our feet, all the world is set in order. Hollywood is full of movies with female characters that believe the message that only a man completes them. The truth is that we are complete in Christ according to the apostle Paul.

> *"For in Christ all the fullness of the Deity lives in bodily form, and in Christ you have been brought to fullness. He is the head over every power and authority"*. (Colossians 2:9-10 NIV)

I remember, vividly, the look on my husband's face when we were dating. We had been talking of marriage, and one night I blurted out, "I just want someone to take care of me!" The look on his face is still before me. That is a really tall order for one person to fill. I was placing all my security and hope in him as a man, when I should have been placing all my trust in God to take care of me. God still uses people to do that, but my point is that my unrealistic expectation placed a burden on my husband that he was never designed to carry. I was holding him responsible for my happiness and care. I was clueless that as a human, one day, he would fail me.

When we hold other people, our spouse, family or friends, responsible for our happiness and provision, we really set ourselves up for disappointment and failure. People will always let you down. There is only One who will not...your heavenly Father. In Christ, He reconciled you back to Himself, so that you could have full dependence on Him to provide for all of your needs. His name tells us that. He is the great I AM. Whatever you have need of, turn to the One who knit you together inside your mother's womb. He will complete you, fill you and take care of all of your needs.

I carry a tattered piece of paper in my bible at all times to remind myself of God's promises to reestablish *all of me*. On it is written the following Word:

- ~ He restores my soul (Psalm 23)
- ~ He keeps my soul (Psalm 121)
- ~ He heals my soul (Isaiah 61)
- ~ He comforts my soul (Isaiah 61)
- ~ He knows and understands my soul (Psalm 139)
- ~ He allows my soul to live (Psalm 119)
- ~ He will not allow my soul to be destroyed (Psalm 16)
- ~ He converts and changes my soul (Psalm 19)

"Praise the LORD, my soul; all my inmost being, praise His holy name." *(Psalm 103:1NKJV)*

Our purpose is to grow in the knowledge of who God is and be filled with all His understanding for our life. As you read most of the New Testament, you see the apostles praying for the believers to be filled with all the essence of who God is. You first purpose is to know God, experience Him and be filled with Him. Out of that understanding, you will be set on a trajectory of what your unique purpose is here on this earth.

"....and we do not cease to pray for you, and to ask that you may be filled with the knowledge of His will in all wisdom and spiritual understanding; that you may walk worthy of the Lord, fully pleasing Him, being fruitful in every good work and increasing in the knowledge of God; strengthened with all might, according to His glorious power, for all patience and longsuffering with joy...."
(Colossians (1:9-11 NKJV)

Paul was praying for the followers of Christ to have four distinct things.
~ to be filled with the knowledge of God
~ to walk worthy of Christ
~ to please Him and be fruitful in goods works
~ to be strengthened with might

The end result of all these actions is patience and joy. I want to be filled with so much joy that it overflows and spills out to others!

This is our purpose, my friend, and hopefully your passion as well. I encourage you to pray the prayer of Colossians, chapter one, over yourself daily and see what happens. God's Word will not be void over your life; it will accomplish more than you ever hoped or dreamed. Take the challenge and stand back and watch your life transform.

When Christ told us that it was for freedom that we have been set free, He was telling us that freedom has been provided for us legally, but it is up to us to *experience* the freedom that He died to give us. If you have struggled to comprehend this reality, it is important to come into agreement with His truths today. My prayer for you is what Paul prayed for the believers in Galatia, that *Christ would be formed IN you.* (Galatians 4:19)

This means that your character becomes conformed into the character of Christ in reality, not merely in appearance. He literally becomes a part of your soul, body and spirit.

Journal

A New Time and A New Place
9
The promise of truth and peace

> "A time to embrace,
> And a time to refrain from embracing;
> A time to gain,
> And a time lose,
> A time to keep,
> And a time to throw away."
> *(Ecclesiastes 3:5b-6 NKJV)*

If you would have asked me several years ago if I wanted to do great and wonderful things for God, I would have emphatically stated, "Absolutely!" However, today if you asked me that same question I would reply differently. I have resigned to the fact that I need only consecrate myself to Him and sit back and watch what only HE can do. I have realized that God will do bigger things through a heart that is, simply, yielded to Him than all the striving we can muster up.

> *"Just relax and let God be God."*
> ~Joyce Meyer

It is really all about surrender, which means to *yield, give up or over, submit, abandon, relinquish, cede, waive, or capitulate.* The surrender of your heart, body, and soul to God is an ongoing process that begins the moment one is born again as a child of God and continues until we leave this earth.

When we continue looking toward others for the key or power to set us free, we will never find it. Mainly, because they don't have it! We must turn to Jesus – only He can unlock all our potential and open the doors to freedom!

What we have vision to see, we can have faith to believe. The power of vision can accelerate the divine and miraculous in your life. A great example of this was Jesus' mother, Mary. At the wedding in Cana, found in John 2:1-10, we see a dilemma. The wedding party had run out of wine and Mary turns to Jesus for the solution. Jesus replied that "his hour had not yet come…." and appears to do nothing. Instantly, we see Mary take action. I am certain that she perceived inside of her son His divine power and activated her faith to ask for a miracle. As a result, we see the unfolding of the story where common water is, indeed, turned into wine.

Faith can sometimes be produced by our vision. What are you seeing today? Faith that sees has the ability to reach into the future and pull it down, into the *now*.

Sometimes we don't realize what will flow out of our choices in the desert crossroads of our life. As we make up our mind about life's direction, a simple decision can be the one element that causes our life to flower and bear fruit. Sometimes the strength of that one commitment can bring you to a new time and a new place...and a new passion for life. Like the wedding in Cana, it can also produce miracles!

Before the rewards, however, there is commitment. Before the blessings and bounty occur, we must make the naked decision to follow the God of the Universe...no matter where...no matter what.

Have you ever said these words? *"Oh... if I could only find the will of God! If I could only be sure of getting hold of His will!"*

Yet the will of God is found in your heart, we only need to tap into what is already there. I believe this is what Jesus was referring to in the book of John.

"Anyone who believes in me may come and drink! For the Scriptures declare, 'Rivers of living water will flow from his heart."
(John 7:38 NLT)

You can get good counsel and read helpful books and diagram your life on the kitchen table but ultimately, the answer is in your heart. When your heart is totally given over to follow Christ and you walk in His ways, you can't miss the will of God in the outworking of your daily life. He'll get your feet there, one way or another. Yes, the route may be roundabout. It might include a climb over some jagged mountains and dip down through some dry, rocky valleys, but trust that He will get you there.

I love the story of Blind Bartemaeus, found in the book of Luke 18:35-43. I encourage you to read it and meditate on its truths. For the sake of brevity, I will paraphrase it for you.

Jesus and His followers are walking along a dusty, narrow road on the way to Jericho. As Jesus passed, he crossed in front of a blind man begging. His name was Bartemaeus, and when he heard the multitudes passing in front of him, he asked who it was. The crowd told him it was Jesus of Nazareth passing through. Immediately, Bartemaeus cries out, "Jesus, Son of David, have mercy on me!" The crowd tells him to be quiet, but Bartimaeus doesn't listen and he begins to cry even louder. His cries reach Jesus' ears and Jesus turns. He commands his friends to bring Bartemaeus to Him.

Jesus asks him a question that almost seems silly, I am sure, as it is quite obvious that the man has no sight. (I believe Jesus wants us to name what it is we have need of). And so, Jesus asks him, "What do you want me to do for you?" Standing before his Lord, Bartimaeus simply states that he wants his sight restored. Scripture tells us that immediately his request was granted. Blind Bartimaeus can now see….where he once was blind, he now has full vision.

What if Bartimaeus had listened to the crowd and quit crying out? What if he chose to remain sitting, soundlessly, on that hot, dusty road, begging? What if he had not gotten out of his comfort zone and tried something different? I believe if he had remained in his present state, he would still be blind. But he didn't! He cried out to the Lord Jesus, with a loud voice, and he didn't let up. He didn't allow the people to stop him from getting his miracle that day.

Cry out to the Lord what you have need of. Cry like Bartimaeus and don't stop until Jesus turns and grants your request. He will because He loves you dearly; just as He loved Bartimaeus, that day long ago.

Daily Declaration

"You will also decree a thing, and it will be established for you; And light will shine on your ways." (Job 22:28 NASB)

There is a supernatural power released when we open our mouth and speak God's Words. God created everything through the power of speaking words. We are created in His image and we, through the blood of Christ, have His authority to speak over our lives and situations. Throughout my life there have been benchmarks I can look at when things shifted dramatically for God's greater good, and it happened when I began to speak His promises and truth.

Below is a daily declaration I began to speak over my life as I was coming out of my own bondage of shame. I hope you can find its worth and choose to decree this goodness over yourself, your marriage and your family. It is the foundation of my life and I pray it will become yours as well.

> In Christ, I am a new creation, and all the old thoughts and behaviors no longer have power over me. I am being renewed every day with God's love and character. I share in God's divine nature because God's Spirit lives in me. I am free from condemnation and have the strength to live my life free of despairing thoughts and the competing desires of my flesh. I am God's workmanship, created to do good works, which God has prepared, ahead of time, for me to accomplish. I am more than a conqueror through God who loves me. I have a clear mind and can make good decisions. I am increasing daily in faith, strength, wisdom, and love. I am able to love others because God has first loved me.

"Whoever desires to save his life will lose it, but whoever loses his life for My sake will find it." *(Matthew 16:25 NKJV)*

Remember, our life is already lost; it is dead and hidden in God. (Colossians 3:3) We belong to Him; we are His. As you journey with God, I promise He will bring great purpose, satisfaction and meaning to your life.

The Japanese believe that when something has suffered damage and has a history it becomes more beautiful. Through the art of Kintsugi, they mend broken objects, aggrandizing the damage by filling the cracks with gold. The damaged vessel now holds value and importance and will be used and displayed as worthy- something to be useful. This is the practice of restoring something to its former glory. It is what God is best at doing. He is the great God of restoration.

 Read Joel 2:25 and write out God's promises:

As we turn our hearts back to Him, God promises to be gracious and merciful. In fact, that is one prayer you will always get answered, "*Lord, have mercy on me!*"

Let's dig a little deeper; answer these questions:

1. What are your spiritual gifts?

2. What kind of character qualities do you have?

3. What is the dream in your heart?

4. What do you value in yourself?

5. What do you value in others?

6. What is your best quality?

7. What do you know about yourself that will never change?

8. What do you need in your life to bring happiness?

Go back and look over your answers as they are a glimpse of your true self. Do you see any patterns or a theme that emerges in your answers?

In Deuteronomy 30:19, The Lord told the children of Israel that He had set before them life and death, blessing and cursing. He then pleads with them to choose life. As you look at your answers, I would say the same to you. Choose LIFE! Choose the things that bring you life and stay away from the choices that limit you, cause you to feel bad and ultimately bring death. Determine how being true to your original design will enable you to live a healthier and happier life.

Read Psalm 139:14-15 and list what your original design looks like.

My final admonition to you is this: Get out into the harvest, dear one. Step outside of yourself like Bartimaeus did and touch lives for Jesus' sake. As you do, things will begin to happen. Without even being aware of it, you'll be edging ever nearer to that new time and place in your life. Your availability becomes God's opportunity to perform the miraculous in and through you. All things are truly possible to the one who dares to believe!

Whether it is as simple as spending time chatting with parents at the bus stop, or phoning friends you haven't seen in a while, or as complicated as organizing a group to serve as volunteers, there are many ways to allow yourself to be used for God's glory. Will you become available today?

> *"Never imagine that what you do for others or what you do in private doesn't matter. It counts more than we know. God watches how we steward what is not our own before He entrusts us with more."*
> ~Lisa Bevere

List a few practical ways you could begin implementing this practice:

Journal

Sow Well 10
Be intentional and reap abundantly

I want to encourage you to cultivate the presence of God in your life. When a farmer gets ready to plant seeds in the ground to enjoy its harvest, he first prepares the soil. He cultivates the soil so it is prepared to receive the seed. There is a spiritual law that operates around us, every day, whether we acknowledge it or believe it. Some call it Karma. Jesus refers to it in the gospels as the law of sowing and reaping.

"A farmer was sowing grain in his fields. As he scattered the seed across the ground, some fell beside a path, and the birds came and ate it. And some fell on rocky soil where there was little depth of earth; the plants sprang up quickly enough in the shallow soil, but the hot sun soon scorched them and they withered and died, for they had so little root. Other seeds fell among thorns, and the thorns choked out the tender blades. But some fell on good soil and produced a crop that was thirty, sixty, and even a hundred times as much as he had planted. If you have ears, listen!" *(Matthew 13:4-9 NLT)*

After Jesus spoke these things, his disciples came and asked why he was speaking to them in hard to understand stories. So Jesus begins to unpack the story for them.

"The hard path where some of the seeds fell represents the heart of a person who hears the Good News about the Kingdom and doesn't understand it; then Satan comes and snatches away the seeds from his heart. The shallow, rocky soil represents the heart of a man who hears the message and receives it with real joy, but he doesn't have much depth in his life, and the seeds don't root very deeply, and after a while when trouble comes, or persecution begins because of his beliefs, his enthusiasm fades, and he drops out. The ground covered with thistles represents a man who hears the message, but the cares of this life and his longing for money choke out God's Word, and he does less and less for God. The good ground represents the heart of a man who listens to the message and understands it and goes out and brings thirty, sixty, or even a hundred others into the Kingdom." (Matthew 13:19-23 TLB)

It is not a matter of whether you are sowing or not – you are. You must consider what you are sowing. Think about your relationships. Are you sowing the seeds of life, and watering with the waters of life?

Paul tells us in the book of Galatians:

> *"Do not be deceived,*
> *God is not mocked;*
> *for whatever a man sows,*
> *that he will also reap."*
> (Galatians 6:7 NKJV)

Step out of all the dishonesty of the past and make out that your life is one big field waiting for the right seeds to be planted. You can start with a small seed of determination to make a change. Every day begin to plant more and more seeds so that in the future you will reap a huge dividend of eternal reward from God.

> **You will never change your life until you change something you do daily."**
> ~John C. Maxwell

Till the soil of your heart, cultivate it, plow it up, fertilize it and apply weed and feed. As you plant the seed of God's truth deep into the soil of your heart, you will begin to uncover your true identity and destiny. Make a conscious decision to build your life on the firm foundation of God's love and truth. Personally, I strive every day to spend time meditating, worshipping and praying before I begin my daily activities.

> *"Guard your heart above all else, for it determines the course of your life."*
> *(Proverbs 4:23 NLT)*

I have grasped the importance of cultivating the presence of God. I allow His love to weed out any and all fears. I allow His love to address the conditions of my heart. Sometimes my heart operates on circumstances or conditions of whether or not I can trust a situation or person. I recognize this, but ultimately I put my trust on the LORD and I am convinced; I will not be shaken.

Jesus had the Spirit without measure. Upon His baptism, the heavens opened up and the Spirit descended upon Him in the form of a dove, and remained. I want the Spirit of God to remain on my person. The truth is that He is within me and His promise is never to leave me or forsake me. Ask yourself the important question; is He resting UPON me? Is there a tangible manifestation of His presence evident in my life?

One day the Pharisees came to Jesus and asked him when the kingdom of God would come. They wanted to know if it was possible to visibly see the realm of God's dominion. This is how He responded:

"The kingdom of God does not come with observation; nor will they say, 'See here!' or 'See there!' For indeed, the kingdom of God is within you." (Luke 17:21 NKJV)

Take heart, my friends, if you have faith in Jesus and what He did, then you carry inside of you everything you need to live an abundant life. Only believe! You and I have been given everything we need for life and godliness, in Christ Jesus. THIS is the great and wonderful news! My prayer is that you will take your life and bundle it up in the totality of HIS life and experience lasting joy, peace and rest.

Shalom.

...And Jesus spoke... "The thief does not come except to steal, and to kill, and to destroy. I have come that they may have life, and that they may have it more abundantly."
(John 10:10 NKJV)

Journal

Epilogue 11

One of my deepest wounds was the rejection from my earthly father. Though I grew up knowing I was conceived out of wedlock and not planned for; my heavenly Father had plans and purposes for me that could not be stopped. An event in my early 20's changed everything for me and my family. I came home from college one weekend to find my dad had gotten born-again. The radical change of his life is what catapulted me on my own journey in knowing God and discovery my true identity. Even in my marriage of 28 years, there have been huge obstacles to overcome. My husband and I have had to face some tough issues that most would run from. It is a good thing we are both strong-willed because instead of throwing in the towel, we picked it up, grabbed hands with Jesus and said, "no matter what, we will do whatever it takes to be whole and free!"

All I can say is, but God! Without His presence, power and love in my life, I am convinced I would not be where I am today. Our three daughters have gotten to see the gospel, up close and personal. Certainly they have been impacted watching their parents trudge through the ugly waters of shame and addiction, but it has been for the upgrading of their own souls. The greatest message our family has lived is knowing and believing that there is power in facing your own shadows. We found that choosing forgiveness really is the better option, because it produces joy and peace. We have seen that God is able to pick up the pieces of the past and reassemble them into a beautiful mosaic. Our family has seen the promise of Joel chapter two... God indeed restores ALL the years that the locusts have eaten and destroyed.

With Him, all things are possible!

Read more by Lisa L. Roitsch by visiting her blog, ministry website or on Facebook at:

- Blog: https://iwillnotstaysilent.wordpress.com

- Personal Ministry Facebook https://www.facebook.com/lisaroitsch/

- Power of His Love Ministries www.powerofhislove.com https://www.facebook.com/powerofhisloveministries/

Made in the USA
Coppell, TX
21 July 2022

80237926R00059